**WHAT I HEARD AB**

# ELIOT WEINBERGER

# WHAT I HEARD ABOUT IRAQ

VERSO

London • New York

First published by Verso 2005

© Eliot Weinberger 2005

All rights reserved

The moral rights of the author have been asserted

1 3 5 7 9 10 8 6 4 2

**Verso**

UK: 6 Meard Street, London WIF OEG
USA: 180 Varick Street, New York, NY 10014-4606
www.versobooks.com
Verso is the imprint of New Left Books

ISBN 1 84467 036 8

**British Library Cataloguing in Publication Data**
A catalogue record for this book
is available from the British Library

**Library of Congress Cataloguing-in-Publication Data**
A catalog record for this book
is available from the Library of Congress

Typeset in Minion by Peter Campbell
Cover design: Peter Campbell
Printed in the UK by The Bath Press

# WHAT I HEARD ABOUT IRAQ

In 1992, a year after the first Gulf War, I heard Dick Cheney, then secretary of defense, say that the US had been wise not to invade Baghdad and get 'bogged down in the problems of trying to take over and govern Iraq.' I heard him say: 'The question in my mind is how many additional American casualties is Saddam worth? And the answer is: not very damned many.'

In February 2001, I heard Colin Powell say that Saddam Hussein 'has not developed any significant capability with respect to weapons of mass destruction. He is unable to project conventional power against his neighbours.'

That same month, I heard that a CIA report stated: 'We do not have any direct evidence that Iraq has used the period since Desert Fox to reconstitute its weapons of mass destruction programmes.'

In July 2001, I heard Condoleezza Rice say: 'We are able to keep his arms from him. His military forces have not been rebuilt.'

On 11 September 2001, six hours after the attacks, I heard that Donald Rumsfeld said that it might be an opportunity to 'hit' Iraq. I heard that he said: 'Go massive. Sweep it all up. Things related and not.'

I heard that Condoleezza Rice asked: 'How do you capitalise on these opportunities?'

I heard that on 17 September the president signed a document marked 'top secret' that directed the Pentagon to begin planning for the invasion and that, some months later, he secretly and illegally diverted $700 million approved by Congress for operations in Afghanistan into preparing for the new battle front.

In February 2002, I heard that an unnamed 'senior military commander' said: 'We are moving military and intelligence personnel and resources out of Afghanistan to get ready for a future war in Iraq.'

I heard the president say that Iraq is 'a threat of unique urgency,' and that there is 'no doubt the Iraqi regime continues to possess and conceal some of the most lethal weapons ever devised.'

I heard the vice president say: 'Simply stated, there is no doubt that Saddam Hussein now has weapons of mass destruction.'

I heard the president tell Congress: 'The danger to our country is grave. The danger to our country is growing. The regime is seeking a nuclear bomb, and with fissile material could build one within a year.'

I heard him say: 'The dangers we face will only worsen from month to month and from year to year. To ignore these threats is to encourage them. Each passing day could be the one on which the Iraqi regime gives anthrax or VX nerve gas or, some day, a nuclear weapon to a terrorist ally.'

I heard the president, in the State of the Union address, say that Iraq was hiding materials sufficient to produce 25,000 litres of anthrax, 38,000 litres of botulinum toxin, and 500 tons of sarin, mustard and nerve gas.

I heard the president say that Iraq had attempted to purchase uranium – later specified as 'yellowcake' uranium oxide from Niger – and thousands of aluminium tubes 'suitable for nuclear weapons production.'

I heard the vice president say: 'We know that he's been absolutely devoted to trying to acquire nuclear weapons, and we believe he has, in fact, reconstituted nuclear weapons.'

I heard the president say: 'Imagine those 19 hijackers with other weapons and other plans, this time armed by Saddam Hussein. It would take one vial, one canister, one crate slipped into this country to bring a day of horror like none we have ever known.'

I heard Donald Rumsfeld say: 'Some have argued that the nuclear threat from Iraq is not imminent. I would not be so certain.'

I heard the president say: 'America must not ignore the threat gathering against us. Facing clear evidence of peril, we cannot wait for the final proof – the smoking gun – that could come in the form of a mushroom cloud.'

I heard Condoleezza Rice say: 'We don't want the "smoking gun" to be a mushroom cloud.'

I heard the American ambassador to the European Union tell the Europeans: 'You had Hitler in Europe and no one really did anything about him. The same type of person is in Baghdad.'

I heard Tony Blair say that there is 'massive evidence of a huge system of clandestine laboratories.'

I heard Colin Powell at the United Nations say: 'They can produce enough dry biological agent in a single month to kill thousands upon thousands of people. Saddam Hussein has never accounted for vast amounts of chemical weaponry: 550 artillery shells with mustard gas, 30,000 empty munitions, and enough precursors to increase his stockpile to as much as 500 tons of chemical agents. Our conservative estimate is that Iraq today has a stockpile of between 100 and 500 tons of chemical-weapons agent. Even the low end of 100 tons of agent would enable Saddam Hussein to cause mass casualties across more than 100 square miles of territory, an area nearly five times the size of Manhattan.'

I heard him say: 'Every statement I make today is backed up by sources, solid sources. These are not assertions. What we're giving you are facts and conclusions based on solid intelligence.'

I heard the president say: 'Iraq has a growing fleet of manned and unmanned aerial vehicles that could be used to disperse chemical or biological weapons across broad areas.' I heard him say that Iraq 'could launch a biological or chemical attack in as little as 45 minutes after the order is given.'

I heard Tony Blair say: 'We are asked to accept Saddam decided to destroy those weapons. I say that such a claim is palpably absurd.'

I heard the president say: 'We know that Iraq and al-Qaida have had high-level contacts that go back a decade. We've learned that Iraq has trained al-Qaida members in bomb-making and poisons and deadly gases. Alliance with terrorists could allow the Iraq regime to attack America without leaving any fingerprints.'

I heard the vice president say: 'There's overwhelming evidence there was a connection between al-Qaida and the Iraqi government. I am very confident there was an established relationship there.'

I heard Colin Powell say: 'Iraqi officials deny accusations of ties with al-Qaida. These denials are simply not credible.'

I heard Condoleezza Rice say: 'There clearly are contacts between al-Qaida and Saddam Hussein that can be documented.'

I heard the president say: 'You can't distinguish between al-Qaida and Saddam.'

I heard Donald Rumsfeld say: 'Imagine a September 11th with weapons of mass destruction. It's not three thousand – it's tens of thousands of innocent men, women and children.'

I heard Colin Powell tell the Senate that 'a

moment of truth is coming': 'This is not just an academic exercise or the United States being in a fit of pique. We're talking about real weapons. We're talking about anthrax. We're talking about botulinum toxin. We're talking about nuclear weapons programmes.'

I heard Donald Rumsfeld say: 'No terrorist state poses a greater or more immediate threat to the security of our people.'

I heard the president, 'bristling with irritation,' say: 'This business about more time, how much time do we need to see clearly that he's not disarming? He is delaying. He is deceiving. He is asking for time. He's playing hide-and-seek with inspectors. One thing is for certain: he's not disarming. Surely our friends have learned lessons from the past. This looks like a rerun of a bad movie and I'm not interested in watching it.'

I heard that, a few days before authorising the invasion of Iraq, the Senate was told in a classified briefing by the Pentagon that Iraq could launch anthrax and other biological and chemical weapons against the eastern seaboard of the United States using unmanned aerial 'drones.'

I heard Donald Rumsfeld say he would present no specific evidence of Iraqi weapons of mass destruction because it might jeopardise the military mission by revealing to Baghdad what the United States knows.

I HEARD the Pentagon spokesman call the military plan 'A-Day,' or 'Shock and Awe.' Three or four hundred cruise missiles launched every day, until 'there will not be a safe place in Baghdad,' until 'you have this simultaneous effect, rather like the nuclear weapons at Hiroshima, not taking days or weeks but in minutes.' I heard the spokesman say: 'You're sitting in Baghdad and all of a sudden you're the general and thirty of your division headquarters have been wiped out. You also take the city down. By that I mean you get rid of their power, water. In two, three, four, five days they are physically, emotionally and psychologically exhausted.' I heard him say: 'The sheer size of this has never been seen before, never contemplated.'

I heard Major-General Charles Swannack promise that his troops were going to 'use a sledgehammer to smash a walnut.'

I heard the Pentagon spokesman say: 'This is not going to be your father's Persian Gulf War.'

I heard that Saddam's strategy against the American invasion would be to blow up dams, bridges and oilfields, and to cut off food supplies to the south so that the Americans would suddenly have to feed millions of desperate civilians. I heard that Baghdad would be encircled by two rings of the elite Republican Guard, in fighting positions already stocked with weapons and supplies, and equipped with chemical protective gear against the poison gas or germ weapons they would be using against the American troops.

I heard Vice Admiral Lowell Jacoby tell Congress that Saddam would 'employ a "scorched earth" strategy, destroying food, transportation, energy and other infrastructure, attempting to create a humanitarian disaster,' and that he would blame it all on the Americans.

I heard that Iraq would fire its long-range Scud missiles – equipped with chemical or biological warheads – at Israel, to 'portray the war as a battle with an American-Israeli coalition and build support in the Arab world.'

I heard that Saddam had elaborate and labyrinthine underground bunkers for his protection, and that it might be necessary to employ B-61 Mod 11 nuclear 'bunker-buster' bombs to destroy them.

I heard the vice president say that the war would be over in 'weeks rather than months.'

I heard Donald Rumsfeld say: 'It could last six days, six weeks. I doubt six months.'

I heard Donald Rumsfeld say there was 'no question' that American troops would be 'welcomed': 'Go back to Afghanistan, the people were in the streets playing music, cheering, flying kites, and doing all the things that the Taliban and al-Qaida would not let them do.'

I heard the vice president say: 'The Middle East expert Professor Fouad Ajami predicts that after liberation the streets in Basra and Baghdad are "sure to erupt in joy." Extremists in the region would have to rethink their strategy of jihad. Moderates throughout the region would take heart. And our ability to advance the Israeli-Palestinian peace process would be enhanced.'

I heard the vice president say: 'I really do believe we will be greeted as liberators.'

I heard Tariq Aziz, the Iraqi foreign minister, say: 'American soldiers will not be received by flowers. They will be received by bullets.'

I heard that the president said to the television evangelist Pat Robertson: 'Oh, no, we're not going to have any casualties.'

I heard the president say that he had not consulted his father about the coming war: 'You know he is the wrong father to appeal to in terms of strength. There is a higher father that I appeal to.'

I heard the prime minister of the Solomon Islands express surprise that his was one of the nations enlisted in the 'coalition of the willing': 'I was completely unaware of it.'

I heard the president tell the Iraqi people, on the night before the invasion began: 'If we must begin a military campaign, it will be directed against the lawless men who rule your country and not against you. As our coalition takes away their power we will deliver the food and medicine you need. We will tear down the apparatus of terror. And we will help you build a new Iraq that is prosperous and free. In a free Iraq there will be no more wars of aggression against your neighbours, no more poison factories, no more executions of dissidents, no more torture chambers and rape rooms. The tyrant will soon be gone. The day of your liberation is near.'

I heard him tell the Iraqi people: 'We will not relent until your country is free.'

I HEARD the vice president say: 'By any standard of even the most dazzling charges in military history, the Germans in the Ardennes in the spring of 1940 or Patton's romp in July of 1944, the present race to Baghdad is unprecedented in its speed and daring and in the lightness of casualties.'

I heard Colonel David Hackworth say: 'Hey diddle diddle, it's straight up the middle!'

I heard the Pentagon spokesman say that 95 per cent of the Iraqi casualties were 'military-age males.'

I heard an official from the Red Crescent say: 'On one stretch of highway alone, there were more than fifty civilian cars, each with four or five people incinerated inside, that sat in the sun for ten or fifteen days before they were buried nearby by volunteers. That is what there will be for their relatives to come and find. War is bad, but its remnants are worse.'

I heard the director of a hospital in Baghdad say: 'The whole hospital is an emergency room. The nature of the injuries is so severe –

one body without a head, someone else with their abdomen ripped open.'

I heard an American soldier say: 'There's a picture of the World Trade Center hanging up by my bed and I keep one in my Kevlar. Every time I feel sorry for these people I look at that. I think: "They hit us at home and now it's our turn."'

I heard about Hashim, a fat, 'painfully shy' 15-year-old, who liked to sit for hours by the river with his birdcage, and who was shot by the 4th Infantry Division in a raid on his village. Asked about the details of the boy's death, the division commander said: 'That person was probably in the wrong place at the wrong time.'

I heard an American soldier say: 'We get rocks thrown at us by kids. You wanna turn around and shoot one of the little fuckers, but you know you can't do that.'

I heard the Pentagon spokesman say that the US did not count civilian casualties: 'Our efforts focus on destroying the enemy's capabilities, so we never target civilians and have no reason to try to count such unintended deaths.' I heard him say that, in any event, it would be impossible, because the Iraqi paramilitaries were fighting in civilian clothes, the military was using civilian human shields, and many of the civilian deaths were the result of Iraqi 'unaimed anti-aircraft fire falling back to earth.'

I heard an American soldier say: 'The worst thing is to shoot one of them, then go help him,' as regulations require. 'Shit, I didn't help any of them. I wouldn't help the fuckers. There were some you let die. And there were some you double-tapped. Once you'd reached the objective, and once you'd shot them and you're moving through, anything there, you shoot again. You didn't want any prisoners of war.'

I heard Anmar Uday, the doctor who had cared for Private Jessica Lynch, say: 'We heard the helicopters. We were surprised. Why do this? There was no military. There were no soldiers in the hospital. It was like a Hollywood film. They cried "Go, go, go," with guns and flares and the sound of explosions.

They made a show: an action movie like Sylvester Stallone or Jackie Chan, with jumping and shouting, breaking down doors. All the time with cameras rolling.'

I heard Private Jessica Lynch say: 'They used me as a way to symbolise all this stuff. It hurt in a way that people would make up stories that they had no truth about.' Of the stories that she had bravely fought off her captors, and suffered bullet and stab wounds, I heard her say: 'I'm not about to take credit for something I didn't do.' Of her dramatic 'rescue,' I heard her say: 'I don't think it happened quite like that.'

I heard the Red Cross say that casualties in Baghdad were so high that the hospitals had stopped counting.

I heard an old man say, after 11 members of his family – children and grandchildren – were killed when a tank blew up their minivan: 'Our home is an empty place. We who are left are like wild animals. All we can do is cry out.'

As the riots and looting broke out, I heard a

man in the Baghdad market say: 'Saddam Hussein's greatest crime is that he brought the American army to Iraq.'

As the riots and looting broke out, I heard Donald Rumsfeld say: 'It's untidy, and freedom's untidy.'

I heard him say: 'I picked up a newspaper today and I couldn't believe it. I read eight headlines that talked about chaos, violence, unrest. And it was just Henny Penny – "the sky is falling". I've never seen anything like it! And here is a country that's being liberated, here are people who are going from being repressed and held under the thumb of a vicious dictator, and they're free. And all this newspaper could do, with eight or ten headlines, they showed a man bleeding, a civilian, who they claimed we had shot – one thing after another. It's just unbelievable.'

And when the National Museum was emptied and the National Library burned down, I heard Donald Rumsfeld say: 'The images you are seeing on television you are seeing over, and over, and over, and it's the same picture of some person walking out of some building with a vase, and you see it twenty times, and you think: "My goodness, were there that many vases? Is it possible that there were that many vases in the whole country?"'

I heard that 10,000 Iraqi civilians were dead.

I HEARD Colin Powell say: 'I'm absolutely sure that there are weapons of mass destruction there and the evidence will be forthcoming. We're just getting it now.'

I heard the president say: 'We'll find them. It'll be a matter of time to do so.'

I heard Donald Rumsfeld say: 'We know where they are. They're in the area around Tikrit and Baghdad, and east, west, south and north, somewhat.'

I heard the US was building 14 'enduring bases,' capable of housing 110,000 soldiers, and I heard Brigadier-General Mark Kimmitt call them 'a blueprint for how we could operate in the Middle East.' I heard that the US was building what would be its largest embassy anywhere in the world.

I heard that it would only be a matter of months before Starbucks and McDonald's opened branches in Baghdad. I heard that HSBC would have cash machines all over the country.

I heard about the trade fairs run by New Bridges Strategies, a consulting firm that promised access to the Iraqi market. I heard one of its partners say: 'Getting the rights to distribute Procter & Gamble would be a gold mine. One well-stocked 7-Eleven could knock out 30 Iraqi stores. A Wal-Mart could take over the country.'

On 1 May 2003, I heard the president, dressed up as a pilot, under a banner that read 'Mission Accomplished,' declare that combat operations were over: 'The battle of Iraq is one victory in a war on terror that began on September the 11th, 2001.' I heard him say: 'The liberation of Iraq is a crucial advance in the campaign against terror. We've removed an ally of al-Qaida, and cut off a source of terrorist funding. And this much is certain: no terrorist network will gain weapons of mass destruction from the Iraqi regime, because the regime is no more. In these 19 months that changed the world, our actions have been focused and deliberate and proportionate to the offence. We have not forgotten the victims of September 11th: the last phone calls, the cold murder of children, the searches in the rubble. With those attacks, the terrorists and their supporters declared war on the United States. And war is what they got.'

On 1 May 2003, I heard that 140 American soldiers had died in combat in Iraq.

I heard Richard Perle tell Americans to 'relax and celebrate victory.' I heard him say: 'The predictions of those who opposed this war can be discarded like spent cartridges.'

I heard Lieutenant-General Jay Garner say: 'We ought to look in a mirror and get proud and stick out our chests and suck in our bellies and say: "Damn, we're Americans."'

And later I heard that I could buy a 12-inch 'Elite Force Aviator: George W. Bush' action figure: 'Exacting in detail and fully equipped with authentic gear, this limited-edition action figure is a meticulous 1:6 scale re-creation of the commander-in-chief's appearance during his historic aircraft carrier landing. This fully poseable figure features a realistic head sculpt, fully detailed cloth flight suit, helmet with oxygen mask, survival vest, G-pants, parachute harness and much more.'

In February 2003, a month before the invasion, I heard General Eric Shinseki tell Congress that 'several hundred thousand troops' would be needed to occupy Iraq. I heard him ridiculed by Paul Wolfowitz as 'wildly off the mark.' I heard that the Secretary of the Army, Thomas White, a former general, was fired for agreeing with Shinseki. In May 2003, I heard that Pentagon planners had predicted that US troop levels would fall to 30,000 by the end of the summer.

I HEARD that Paul Bremer's first act as director of the Coalition Provisional Authority was to fire all senior members of the Baath Party, including 30,000 civil servants, policemen, teachers and doctors, and to dismiss all 400,000 soldiers of the Iraqi army without pay or pensions. Two million people were dependent on that income. Since America supports private gun ownership, the soldiers were allowed to keep their weapons.

I heard that hundreds were being kidnapped and raped in Baghdad alone; that schools, hospitals, shops and factories were being looted; that it was impossible to restore the electricity because all the copper wire was being stolen from the power plants.

I heard Paul Bremer say, 'Most of the country is, in fact, orderly,' and that all the problems were coming from 'several hundred hard-core terrorists' from al-Qaida and affiliated groups.

As attacks on American troops increased, I heard the generals disagree about who was fighting: Islamic fundamentalists or remnants of the Baath Party or Iraqi mercenaries or foreign mercenaries or ordinary citizens taking revenge for the loss of loved ones. I heard the president and the vice president and the politicians and the television reporters simply call them 'terrorists.'

I heard the president say: 'There are some who feel that conditions are such that they can attack us there. My answer is: bring them on! We have the force necessary to deal with the situation.'

I heard that 25,000 Iraqi civilians were dead.

I heard Arnold Schwarzenegger, then campaigning for governor, in Baghdad for a special showing to the troops of *Terminator 3*, say: 'It is really wild driving round here, I mean the poverty, and you see there is no money, it is disastrous financially and there is the leadership vacuum, pretty much like California.'

I heard that the army was wrapping entire villages in barbed wire, with signs that read: 'This fence is here for your protection. Do not approach or try to cross, or you will be shot.'

In one of those villages, I heard a man named Tariq say: 'I see no difference between us and the Palestinians.'

I heard Captain Todd Brown say: 'You have to understand the Arab mind. The only thing they understand is force – force, pride and saving face.'

I heard that the US, as 'a gift from the American people to the Iraqi people,' had committed $18.4 billion to the reconstruction of basic infrastructure, but that future Iraqi governments would have no say in how the money was spent. I heard that the economy had been opened to foreign ownership, and that this could not be changed. I heard that the Iraqi army would be under the command of the US, and that this could not be changed. I heard, however, that 'full authority' for health and hospitals had been turned over to the Iraqis, and that senior American health advisers had been withdrawn. I heard Tommy Thompson, Secretary of Health and Human Services, say that Iraq's hospitals would be fine if the Iraqis 'just washed their hands and cleaned the crap off the walls.'

I heard Colonel Nathan Sassaman say: 'With a heavy dose of fear and violence, and a lot of money for projects, I think we can convince these people that we are here to help them.'

I heard Richard Perle say: 'Next year at about this time, I expect there will be a really thriving trade in the region, and we will see rapid economic development. And a year from now, I'll be very surprised if there is not some grand square in Baghdad named after President Bush.'

I HEARD about Operation Ivy Cyclone. I heard about Operation Vigilant Resolve. I heard about Operation Plymouth Rock. I heard about Operation Iron Hammer, its name taken from Eisenhammer, the Nazi plan to destroy Soviet generating plants.

I heard that air force regulations require that any airstrike likely to result in the deaths of more than 30 civilians be personally approved by the secretary of defense, and I heard that Donald Rumsfeld approved every proposal.

I heard a marine colonel say: 'We napalmed those bridges. Unfortunately, there were people there. It's no great way to die.'

I heard a marine describe 'dead-checking': 'They teach us to do dead-checking when we're clearing rooms. You put two bullets into the guy's chest and one in the brain. But when you enter a room where guys are wounded, you might not know if they're alive or dead. So they teach us to dead-check them by pressing them in the eye with your boot, because generally a person, even if he's faking being dead, will flinch if you poke him there. If he moves, you put a bullet in the brain. You do this to keep the momentum going when you're flowing through a building. You don't want a guy popping up behind you and shooting you.'

I heard the president say: 'We're rolling back the terrorist threat, not on the fringes of its influence but at the heart of its power.'

When the death toll of American soldiers reached 500, I heard Brigadier-General Kimmitt say: 'I don't think the soldiers are looking at arbitrary figures such as casualty counts as the barometer of their morale. They know they have a nation that stands behind them.'

I heard an American soldier, standing next to his Humvee, say: 'We liberated Iraq. Now the people here don't want us here, and guess what? We don't want to be here either. So why are we still here? Why don't they bring us home?'

I heard Colin Powell say: 'We did not expect it would be quite this intense this long.'

I heard Donald Rumsfeld say: 'We're facing a test of will.'

I heard the president say: 'We found biological laboratories. They're illegal. They're against the United Nations resolutions, and we've so far discovered two. And we'll find more weapons as time goes on. But for those who say we haven't found the banned manufacturing devices or banned weapons, they're wrong, we found them.'

I heard Tony Blair say: 'The remains of 400,000 human beings have been found in mass graves.' And I saw his words repeated in a US government pamphlet, *Iraq's Legacy of Terror: Mass Graves*, and on a US government website which said this represented 'a crime against humanity surpassed only by the Rwandan genocide of 1994, Pol Pot's Cambodian killing fields in the 1970s and the Nazi Holocaust of World War Two.'

I HEARD the president say: 'Today, on bended knee, I thank the Good Lord for protecting those of our troops overseas, and our Coalition troops and innocent Iraqis who suffer at the hands of some of these senseless killings by people who are trying to shake our will.'

I heard that this was the first American president in wartime who had never attended a funeral for a dead soldier. I heard that photographs of the flag-draped coffins returning home were banned. I heard that the Pentagon had renamed body bags 'transfer tubes.'

I heard a tearful George Bush Sr, speaking at the annual convention of the National Petrochemical and Refiners Association, say that it was 'deeply offensive and contemptible' the way 'elites and intellectuals' were dismissing 'the sowing of the seeds of basic human freedom in that troubled part of the world.' I heard him say: 'It hurts an awful lot more when it's your son that is being criticised.'

I heard the president's mother say: 'Why should we hear about body bags and deaths? Why should I waste my beautiful mind on something like that?'

I heard that the president and Tony Blair were praying together at Camp David.

I heard that 7 per cent of all American military deaths in Iraq were suicides, that 10 per cent of the soldiers evacuated to the army hospital in Landstuhl, Germany had been sent for 'psychiatric or behavioural health issues,' and that 20 per cent of the military was expected to suffer from post-traumatic stress disorder.

I heard Brigadier-General Kimmitt deny that civilians were being killed: 'We run extremely precise operations.'

I heard Donald Rumsfeld say that the fighting was the work of 'thugs, gangs and terrorists.' I heard General Richard Myers, chairman of the Joint Chiefs of Staff, say: 'It's not a Shiite uprising. Muqtada al-Sadr has a very small following.' I heard that an unnamed 'intelligence official' said: 'Hatred of the

American occupation has spread rapidly among Shia, and is now so large that Mr Sadr and his forces represent just one element. Destroying his Mehdi Army might be possible only by destroying Sadr City.' Sadr City is the most populated part of Baghdad. I heard that, among the Sunnis, former Baath Party leaders and Saddam loyalists had been joined by Sunni tribal chiefs.

I heard that there were now thirty separate militias in the country. I heard the television news reporters routinely refer to them as 'anti-Iraqi forces.'

I heard that Paul Bremer had closed down a popular newspaper, *Al Hawza*, because of 'inaccurate reporting.'

As Shias in Sadr City lined up to donate blood for Sunnis in Fallujah, I heard a man say: 'We should thank Paul Bremer. He has finally united Iraq – against him.'

I heard the president say: 'I wouldn't be happy if I were occupied either.'

I HEARD Tony Blair say: 'Before people crow about the absence of weapons of mass destruction, I suggest they wait a bit.'

I heard General Myers say: 'Given time, given the number of prisoners now that we're interrogating, I'm confident that we're going to find weapons of mass destruction.'

I heard the president say: 'Prisoners are being taken, and intelligence is being gathered. Our decisive actions will continue until these enemies of democracy are dealt with.'

I heard a soldier describe what they called 'bitch in a box': 'That was the normal procedure for them when they wanted to soften up a prisoner: stuff them in the trunk for a while and drive them around. The hoods I can understand, and to have them cuffed with the plastic things – that I could see. But the trunk episode – I thought it was kind of unusual. It was like a sweatbox, let's face it. In Iraq, in August, it's hitting 120 degrees, and you can imagine what it was like in the trunk of a black Mercedes.'

I heard a National Guardsman from Florida say: 'We had a sledgehammer that we would bang against the wall, and that would create an echo that sounds like an explosion that scared the hell out of them. If that didn't work we would load a 9mm pistol, and pretend to be charging it near their head and make them think we were going to shoot them. Once you did that they did whatever you wanted them to do basically. The way we treated these men was hard even for the soldiers, especially after realising that many of these "combatants" were no more than shepherds.'

I heard a marine at Camp Whitehorse say: 'The 50/10 technique was used to break down EPWs and make it easier for the HET member to get information from them.' The 50/10 technique was to make prisoners stand for 50 minutes of the hour for ten hours with a hood over their heads in the heat. EPWs were 'enemy prisoners of war.' HETs were 'human exploitation teams.'

I heard Captain Donald Reese, a prison warden, say: 'It was not uncommon to see people without clothing. I was told the "whole nudity thing" was an interrogation procedure used by military intelligence, and never thought much about it.'

I heard Donald Rumsfeld say: 'I have not seen anything thus far that says that the people abused were abused in the process of interrogating them or for interrogation purposes.'

I heard Private Lynndie England, who was photographed in Abu Ghraib holding a prisoner on a leash, say: 'I was instructed by persons in higher rank to stand there, hold this leash, look at the camera, and they took pictures for PsyOps. I didn't really, I mean, want to be in any pictures. I thought it was kind of weird.'

Detainees 27, 30 and 31 were stripped of their clothing, handcuffed together nude, placed on the ground, and forced to lie on each other and simulate sex while photographs were taken. Detainee 8 had his food thrown in the toilet and was then ordered to eat it. Detainee 7 was ordered to bark like a dog while MPs spat and urinated on him; he was sodomised with a police stick while two female MPs watched. Detainee 3 was sodomised with a broom by a female soldier. Detainee 15 was photographed standing on a box with a hood on his head and simulated electrical wires attached to his hands and penis. Detainees 1, 16, 17, 18, 23, 24 and 26 were placed in a pile and forced to masturbate while photographs were taken. An unidentified detainee was photographed covered in faeces with a banana inserted in his anus. Detainee 5 watched Civilian 1 rape an unidentified 15-year-old male detainee while a female soldier took photographs. Detainees 5 and 7 were stripped of their clothing and forced to wear women's underwear on their heads. Detainee 28, handcuffed with his hands behind his back in a shower stall, was declared dead when an MP removed the sandbag from his head and checked his pulse.

I heard Donald Rumsfeld say: 'If you are in Washington DC, you can't know what's going on in the midnight shift in one of those many prisons around the world.'

I HEARD that the Red Cross had to close its offices because it was too dangerous. I heard that General Electric and the Siemens Corporation had to close their offices. I heard that Médecins sans Frontières had to withdraw, and that journalists rarely left their hotels. I heard that, after their headquarters were bombed, most of the United Nations staff had gone. I heard that the cost of life insurance policies for the few remaining Western businessmen was $10,000 a week.

I heard Tom Foley, director of Iraq Private Sector Development, say: 'The security risks are not as bad as they appear on TV. Western civilians are not the targets themselves. These are acceptable risks.'

I heard the spokesman for Paul Bremer say: 'We have isolated pockets where we are encountering problems.'

I heard that, no longer able to rely on the military for help, private security firms had banded together to form the largest private army in the world, with its own rescue teams and intelligence. I heard that there were 20,000 mercenary soldiers, now called 'private contractors,' in Iraq, earning as much as $2000 a day, and not subject to Iraqi or US military law.

I heard that 50,000 Iraqi civilians were dead.

I heard that, on a day when a car bomb killed three Americans, Paul Bremer's last act as director of the Coalition Provisional Authority was to issue laws making it illegal to drive with only one hand on the steering wheel or to honk a horn when there was no emergency.

I heard that the unemployment rate was now 70 per cent, that less than 1 per cent of the workforce was engaged in reconstruction, and that the US had spent only 2 per cent of the $18.4 billion approved by Congress for reconstruction. I heard that an official audit could not account for $8.8 billion of Iraqi oil money given to Iraqi ministries by the Coalition Provisional Authority.

I heard the president say: 'Our Coalition is standing with responsible Iraqi leaders as they establish growing authority in their country.'

I heard Tony Blair say: 'Let me make it 100 per cent clear, after June 30 there will be the full transfer of sovereignty to the Iraqi government. If there is a political decision as to whether you go into a place like Fallujah in a particular way, that has to be done with the consent of the Iraqi government and the final political control remains with the Iraqi government.'

I heard that, a few days before he became prime minister, Iyad Allawi visited a Baghdad police station where six suspected insurgents, blindfolded and handcuffed, were lined up against a wall. I heard that, as four Americans and a dozen Iraqi policemen watched, Allawi pulled out a pistol and shot each prisoner in the head. I heard that he said that this is how we must deal with insurgents. I heard that this story was not true, and then heard that even if it weren't true, it was believable.

On 28 June 2004, with the establishment of an interim government, I heard the vice president say: 'After decades of rule by a brutal dictator, Iraq has been returned to its rightful owners, the people of Iraq.'

This was the military summary for an
ordinary day, 22 July 2004, a day that produced
no headlines: 'Two roadside bombs exploded
next to a van and a Mercedes in separate areas
of Baghdad, killing four civilians. A gunman in
a Toyota opened fire on a police checkpoint
and escaped. Police wounded three gunmen at
a checkpoint and arrested four men suspected
of attempted murder. Seven more roadside
bombs exploded in Baghdad and gunmen
twice attacked US troops. Police dismantled a
car bomb in Mosul and gunmen attacked the
Western driver of a gravel truck at Tell Afar.
There were three roadside bombings and a
rocket attack on US troops in Mosul and
another gun attack on US forces near Tell Afar.
At Taji, a civilian vehicle collided with a US
military vehicle, killing six civilians and
injuring seven others. At Bayji, a US vehicle
hit a landmine. Gunmen murdered a dentist
at the Ad Dwar hospital. There were 17
roadside bomb explosions against US forces in
Taji, Baquba, Baqua, Jalula, Tikrit, Paliwoda,
Balad, Samarra and Duluiyeh, with attacks by
gunmen on US troops in Tikrit and Balad.
A headless body in an orange jumpsuit was
found in the Tigris; believed to be Bulgarian

hostage Ivalyo Kepov. Kirkuk air base attacked. Five roadside bombs on US forces in Rutbah, Kalso and Ramadi. Gunmen attacked Americans in Fallujah and Ramadi. The police chief of Najaf was abducted. Two civilian contractors were attacked by gunmen at Haswah. A roadside bomb exploded near Kerbala and Hillah. International forces were attacked by gunmen at al-Qurnah.'

I HEARD the president say: 'You can embolden an enemy by sending a mixed message. You can dispirit the Iraqi people by sending mixed messages. That's why I will continue to lead with clarity and in a resolute way.'

I heard the president say: 'Today, because the world acted with courage and moral clarity, Iraqi athletes are competing in the Olympic Games.' Iraq had sent teams to the previous Olympics. And when the president ran a campaign advertisement with the flags of Iraq and Afghanistan and the words 'At this Olympics there will be two more free nations – and two fewer terrorist regimes,' I heard the Iraqi coach say: 'Iraq as a team does not want Mr Bush to use us for the presidential campaign. He can find another way to advertise himself.' I heard their star midfielder say that if he weren't playing soccer he'd be fighting for the resistance in Fallujah: 'Bush has committed so many crimes. How will he meet his god having slaughtered so many men and women?'

I heard an unnamed 'senior British army

officer' invoke the Nazis to describe what he saw: 'My view and the view of the British chain of command is that the Americans' use of violence is not proportionate and is over-responsive to the threat they are facing. They don't see the Iraqi people the way we see them. They view them as Untermenschen. They are not concerned about the Iraqi loss of life. As far as they are concerned, Iraq is bandit country and everybody is out to kill them. It is trite, but American troops do shoot first and ask questions later.'

I heard Makki al-Nazzal, who was managing a clinic in Fallujah, say, in unaccented English: 'I have been a fool for 47 years. I used to believe in European and American civilisation.'

I heard Donald Rumsfeld say: 'We never believed that we'd just tumble over weapons of mass destruction.'

I heard Condoleezza Rice say: 'We never expected we were going to open garages and find them.'

I heard Donald Rumsfeld say: 'They may have

had time to destroy them, and I don't know
the answer.'

I heard Richard Perle say: 'We don't know
where to look for them and we never did know
where to look for them. I hope this will take
less than two hundred years.'

I HEARD the president say: 'I know what I'm doing when it comes to winning this war.'

I heard the president say: 'I'm a war president.'

I heard that 1000 American soldiers were dead and 7000 wounded in combat. I heard that there was now an average of 87 attacks on US troops a day.

I heard Condoleezza Rice say: 'Not everything has gone as we would have liked it to.'

I heard Colin Powell say: 'We did miscalculate the difficulty.'

I heard an unnamed 'senior US diplomat in Baghdad' say: 'We're dealing with a population that hovers between bare tolerance and outright hostility. This idea of a functioning democracy is crazy. We thought there would be a reprieve after sovereignty, but all hell is breaking loose.'

I heard Major Thomas Neemeyer say: 'The

only way to stomp out the insurgency of the mind would be to kill the entire population.'

I heard the CNN reporter near the tomb of Ali in Najaf, a city that once held 500,000 people, say: 'Everything outside of the mosque seems to be totalled.'

I heard Khudeir Salman, who sold ice from a donkey cart in Najaf, say he was giving up after marine snipers had killed his friend, another ice-seller: 'I found him this morning. The sniper shot his donkey too. Even the ambulance drivers are too scared to get the body.'

I heard the vice president say: 'Such an enemy cannot be deterred, cannot be contained, cannot be appeased, or negotiated with. It can only be destroyed. And that is the business at hand.'

I heard a 'senior American commander' say: 'We need to make a decision on when the cancer of Fallujah needs to be cut out.'

I heard Major-General John Batiste, outside

Samarra, say: 'It'll be a quick fight and the enemy is going to die fast. The message for the people of Samarra is: peacefully or not, this is going to be solved.'

I heard Brigadier-General Kimmitt say: 'Our patience is not eternal.'

I heard the president say: 'America will never be run out of Iraq by a bunch of thugs and killers.'

I heard about the wedding party that was attacked by American planes, killing 45 people, and the wedding photographer who videotaped the festivities until he himself was killed. And though the tape was shown on television, I heard Brigadier-General Kimmitt say: 'There was no evidence of a wedding. There may have been some kind of celebration. Bad people have celebrations, too.'

I heard an Iraqi man say: 'I swear I saw dogs eating the body of a woman.'

I heard an Iraqi man say: 'We have at least 700 dead. So many of them are children and women. The stench from the dead bodies in parts of the city is unbearable.'

I heard Donald Rumsfeld say: 'Death has a tendency to encourage a depressing view of war.'

ON THE OCCASION of Iyad Allawi's visit to the United States, I heard the president say: 'What's important for the American people to hear is reality. And the reality is right here in the form of the prime minister.'

Asked about ethnic tensions, I heard Iyad Allawi say: 'There are no problems between Shia and Sunnis and Kurds and Arabs and Turkmen. Usually we have no problems of an ethnic or religious nature in Iraq.'

I heard him say: 'There is nothing, no problem, except in a small pocket in Fallujah.'

I heard Colonel Jerry Durrant say, after a meeting with Ramadi tribal sheikhs: 'A lot of these guys have read history, and they said to me the government in Baghdad is like the Vichy government in France during World War Two.'

I heard a journalist say: 'I am housebound. I leave when I have a very good reason to and a scheduled interview. I avoid going to people's homes and never walk in the streets. I can't go grocery shopping any more, can't eat in restaurants, can't strike up a conversation with strangers, can't look for stories, can't drive in anything but a full armoured car, can't go to scenes of breaking news stories, can't be stuck in traffic, can't speak English outside, can't take a road trip, can't say "I'm an American," can't linger at checkpoints, can't be curious about what people are saying, doing, feeling.'

I heard Donald Rumsfeld say: 'It's a tough part of the world. We had something like 200 or 300 or 400 people killed in many of the major cities of America last year. What's the difference? We just didn't see each homicide in every major city in the United States on television every night.'

I heard that 80,000 Iraqi civilians were dead. I heard that the war had already cost $225 billion and was continuing at the rate of $40 billion a month. I heard there was now an average of 130 attacks on US troops a day.

I heard Captain John Mountford say: 'I just wonder what would have happened if we had worked a little more with the locals.'

I heard that, in the last year alone, the US had fired 127 tons of depleted uranium (DU) munitions in Iraq, the atomicity equivalent of approximately ten thousand Nagasaki bombs. I heard that the widespread use of DU in the first Gulf War was believed to be the primary cause of the health problems suffered by its 580,400 veterans. 467 were wounded in the war. Ten years later, 11,000 were dead and 325,000 on medical disability. DU carried in semen led to high rates of endometriosis in their wives and girlfriends, often requiring hysterectomies. Of soldiers who had healthy babies before the war, 67 per cent of their postwar babies were born with severe defects, including missing legs, arms, organs or eyes.

I heard that 380 tons of HMX (high melting point explosive) and RDX (rapid detonation explosive) were missing from al-Qaqaa, one of Iraq's 'most sensitive military installations,' which had not been guarded since the invasion. I heard that one pound of these explosives was enough to blow up a 747 jet, and that this cache could be used to make a million roadside bombs, which were the cause of half the casualties among US troops.

I heard Donald Rumsfeld say, when asked why the troops were being kept in the war much longer than their normal tours of duty: 'Oh, come on. People are fungible. You can have them here or there.'

I HEARD Colonel Gary Brandl say: 'The enemy has got a face. He's called Satan. He's in Fallujah and we're going to destroy him.'

I heard a marine commander tell his men: 'You will be held accountable for the facts not as they are in hindsight but as they appeared to you at the time. If, in your mind, you fire to protect yourself or your men, you are doing the right thing. It doesn't matter if later on we find out you wiped out a family of unarmed civilians.'

I heard Lieutenant-Colonel Mark Smith say: 'We're going out where the bad guys live, and we're going to slay them in their zip code.'

I heard that 15,000 US troops invaded Fallujah as planes dropped 500-pound bombs on 'insurgent targets.' I heard they destroyed the Nazzal Emergency Hospital in the centre of the city, killing 20 doctors. I heard they occupied Fallujah General Hospital, which the military had called a 'centre of propaganda' for reporting civilian casualties. I heard that they confiscated all mobile phones and refused to allow doctors and ambulances to go out and help the wounded. I heard they bombed the power plant to black out the city, and that the water was shut off. I heard that every house and shop had a large red X spray-painted on the door to indicate that it had been searched.

I heard Donald Rumsfeld say: 'Innocent civilians in that city have all the guidance they need as to how they can avoid getting into trouble. There aren't going to be large numbers of civilians killed and certainly not by US forces.'

I heard that, in a city of 150 mosques, there were no longer any calls to prayer.

I heard Muhammad Abboud tell how, unable to leave his house to go to a hospital, he had watched his nine-year-old son bleed to death, and how, unable to leave his house to go to a cemetery, he had buried his son in the garden.

I heard Sami al-Jumaili, a doctor, say: 'There is not a single surgeon in Fallujah. A 13-year-old child just died in my hands.'

I heard an American soldier say: 'We will win the hearts and minds of Fallujah by ridding the city of insurgents. We're doing that by patrolling the streets and killing the enemy.'

I heard an American soldier, a Bradley gunner, say: 'I was basically looking for any clean walls, you know, without any holes in them. And then we were putting holes in them.'

I heard Farhan Salih say: 'My kids are hysterical with fear. They are traumatised by the sound but there is nowhere to take them.'

I heard that the US troops allowed women and children to leave the city, but that all 'military age males,' men from 15 to 60, were required to stay. I heard that no food or medicine was allowed into the city.

I heard the Red Cross say that at least 800 civilians had died. I heard Iyad Allawi say there were no civilian casualties in Fallujah.

I heard a man named Abu Sabah say: 'They used these weird bombs that put up smoke like a mushroom cloud. Then small pieces fall from the air with long tails of smoke behind them.' I heard him say that pieces of these bombs exploded into large fires that burned the skin even when water was thrown on it. I heard him say: 'People suffered so much from these.'

I heard Kassem Muhammad Ahmed say: 'I watched them roll over wounded people in the streets with tanks. This happened so many times.'

I heard a man named Khalil say: 'They shot women and old men in the streets. Then they shot anyone who tried to get their bodies.'

I heard Nihida Kadhim, a housewife, say that when she was finally allowed to return to her home, she found a message written with lipstick on her living-room mirror: FUCK IRAQ AND EVERY IRAQI IN IT.

I heard General John Sattler say that the destruction of Fallujah had 'broken the back of the insurgency.'

I heard that three-quarters of Fallujah had

been shelled into rubble. I heard an American soldier say: 'It's kind of bad we destroyed everything, but at least we gave them a chance for a new start.'

I heard that only five roads into Fallujah would remain open. The rest would be sealed with 'sand berms,' mountains of earth. At the entry points, everyone would be photographed, fingerprinted and have iris scans taken before being issued identification cards. All citizens would be required to wear identification cards in plain sight at all times. No private automobiles – the vehicle of suicide bombings – would be allowed in the city. All males would be organised into 'work brigades' rebuilding the city. They would be paid, but participation would be compulsory.

I heard Muhammad Kubaissy, a shopkeeper, say: 'I am still searching for what they have been calling democracy.'

I heard a soldier say that he had talked to his priest about killing Iraqis, and that his priest had told him it was all right to kill for his government as long as he did not enjoy it.

After he had killed at least four men, I heard
the soldier say that he had begun to have
doubts: 'Where the fuck did Jesus say it's OK
to kill people for your government?'

I HEARD Donald Rumsfeld say: 'I don't believe anyone that I know in the administration ever said that Iraq had nuclear weapons.'

I heard Donald Rumsfeld say: 'The Coalition did not act in Iraq because we had discovered dramatic new evidence of Iraq's pursuit of weapons of mass destruction. We acted because we saw the evidence in a dramatic new light, through the prism of our experience on 9/11.'

I heard a reporter say to Donald Rumsfeld: 'Before the war in Iraq, you stated the case very eloquently and you said they would welcome us with open arms.' And I heard Rumsfeld interrupt him: 'Never said that. Never did. You may remember it well, but you're thinking of somebody else. You can't find, anywhere, me saying anything like those things you just said I said.'

I heard Ahmed Chalabi, who had supplied most of the information about the weapons of mass destruction, shrug and say: 'We are heroes in error . . . What was said before is not important.'

I heard Paul Wolfowitz say: 'For bureaucratic reasons, we settled on one issue, weapons of mass destruction, as justification for invading Iraq, because it was the one reason everyone could agree on.'

I heard Condoleezza Rice continue to insist: 'It's not as if anybody believes that Saddam Hussein was without weapons of mass destruction.'

I heard Tony Blair say: 'We know that Saddam Hussein had weapons of mass destruction, and we know that we haven't found them, that we may not find them. But what I wouldn't accept is that he was not a threat, and a threat in WMD terms.'

I heard that the Niger 'yellowcake' uranium was a hoax legitimised by British intelligence, that the aluminium tubes could not be used for nuclear weapons, that the mobile biological laboratories produced hydrogen for weather balloons, that the fleet of unmanned aerial drones was a single broken-down oversized model airplane, that Saddam had no elaborate underground bunkers, that Colin Powell's primary source, his 'solid information' for the evidence he presented at the United Nations, was a paper written ten years before by a graduate student. I heard that, of the 400,000 bodies buried in mass graves, only 5000 had been found.

I heard Lieutenant-General James Conway say: 'It was a surprise to me then, and it remains a surprise to me now, that we have not uncovered weapons. It's not from lack of trying.'

I heard a reporter ask Donald Rumsfeld: 'If they did not have WMDs, why did they pose an immediate threat to this country?' I heard Rumsfeld answer: 'You and a few other critics are the only people I've heard use the phrase "immediate threat." It's become a kind of folklore that that's what happened. If you have any citations, I'd like to see them.' And I heard the reporter read: 'No terrorist state poses a greater or more immediate threat to the security of our people.' Rumsfeld replied: 'It –

my view of – of the situation was that he – he
had – we – we believe, the best intelligence
that we had and other countries had and that
– that we believed and we still do not know –
we will know.'

I heard Sa'adoon al-Zubaydi, an interpreter
who lived in the presidential palace, say: 'For at
least three years Saddam Hussein had been
tired of the day-to-day management of his
regime. He could not stand it any more:
meetings, commissions, dispatches, telephone
calls. So he withdrew . . . Alone, isolated, out
of it. He preferred shutting himself up in his
office, writing novels.'

I HEARD the president say that Iraq is a 'catastrophic success.'

I heard Donald Rumsfeld say: 'They haven't won a single battle the entire time since the end of major combat operations.'

I heard that hundreds of schools had been completely destroyed and thousands looted, and that most people thought it too dangerous to send their children to school. I heard there was no system of banks. I heard that in the cities there were only ten hours of electricity a day and that only 60 per cent of the population had access to drinkable water. I heard that the malnutrition of children was now far worse than in Uganda or Haiti. I heard that none of the 270,000 babies born after the start of the war had received immunisations.

I heard General Muhammad Abdullah Shahwani, the chief of Iraqi intelligence, say that there were now 200,000 active fighters in the insurgency.

I heard Donald Rumsfeld say: 'I don't believe it's our job to reconstruct that country. The

Iraqi people are going to have to reconstruct that country over a period of time.' I heard him say that, in any event, 'the infrastructure of that country was not terribly damaged by the war at all.'

I heard that the American ambassador, John Negroponte, had requested that $3.37 billion intended for water, sewage and electricity projects be transferred to security and oil output.

I heard that the reporters from the al-Jazeera network were indefinitely banned. I heard Donald Rumsfeld say: 'What al-Jazeera is doing is vicious, inaccurate and inexcusable.'

I heard that Spain left the Coalition of the Willing. Hungary left; the Dominican Republic left; Nicaragua left; Honduras left. I heard that the Philippines had left early, after a Filipino truck driver was kidnapped and executed. Norway left. Portugal, Singapore and Tonga left. Poland, Ukraine and the Netherlands said they were leaving. Thailand said it was leaving. Bulgaria was reducing its few hundred troops.

Moldova first cut its force from 42 to 12, and then left.

I heard that the president had once said: 'Two years from now, only the Brits may be with us. At some point, we may be the only ones left. That's OK with me. We are America.'

I heard a reporter ask Lieutenant-General Jay Garner how long the troops would remain in Iraq, and I heard him reply: 'I hope they're there a long time.'

I heard General Tommy Franks say: 'One has to think about the numbers. I think we will be engaged with our military in Iraq for perhaps three, five, perhaps ten years.'

I heard that the Pentagon was now exploring what it called the 'Salvador option,' modelled on the death squads in El Salvador in the 1980s, when John Negroponte was ambassador to Honduras and when Elliott Abrams, now White House adviser on the Middle East, called the massacre at El Mazote 'nothing but Communist propaganda.' Under the plan, the US would advise, train and support paramilitaries in assassination and kidnapping, including secret raids across the Syrian border. In the vice presidential debate, I heard the vice president say: 'Twenty years ago we had a similar situation in El Salvador. We had a guerrilla insurgency that controlled roughly a third of the country . . . And today El Salvador is a whale of a lot better.'

I heard that 100,000 Iraqi civilians were dead. I heard that there was now an average of 150 attacks on US troops a day. I heard that in Baghdad 700 people were being killed every month in 'non-war-related' criminal activities. I heard that 1400 American soldiers had been killed and that the true casualty figure was approximately 25,000.

I heard that Donald Rumsfeld had a machine sign his letters of condolence to the families of soldiers who had been killed. When this caused a small scandal, I heard him say: 'I have directed that in the future I sign each letter.'

I heard the president say: 'The credibility of this country is based upon our strong desire to make the world more peaceful, and the world is now more peaceful.'

I heard the president say: 'I want to be the peace president. The next four years will be peaceful years.'

I heard Attorney General John Ashcroft say, on the day of his resignation: 'The objective of securing the safety of Americans from crime and terror has been achieved.'

I heard the president say: 'For a while we were marching to war. Now we're marching to peace.'

I heard that the US military had purchased 1,500,000,000 bullets for use in the coming year. That is 58 bullets for every Iraqi adult and child.

I heard that Saddam Hussein, in solitary confinement, was spending his time writing poetry, reading the Koran, eating cookies and muffins, and taking care of some bushes and shrubs. I heard that he had placed a circle of white stones around a small plum tree.